T0012562

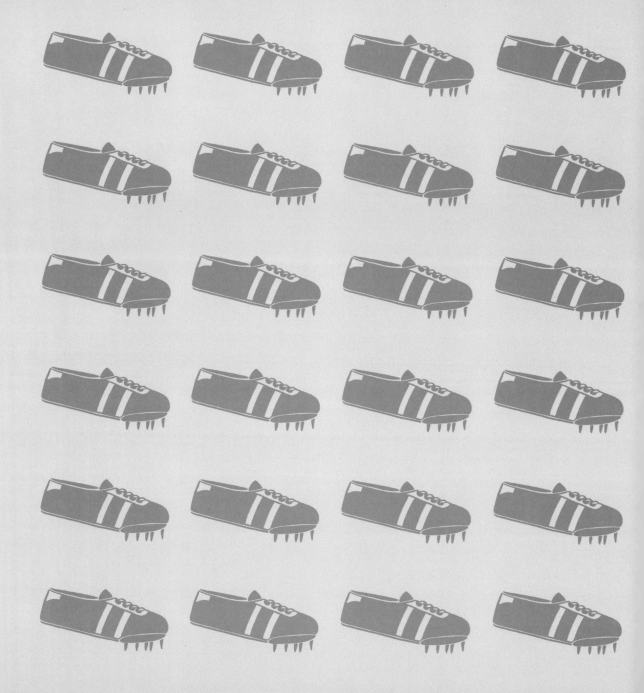

ORDINARY
PEOPLE
CHANGE
— THE —
WORLD

I am Jesse Owens

ON YOUR MARK...

GET SET...

BRAD MELTZER

illustrated by **Christopher Eliopoulos**

 ROCKY POND BOOKS

I am JESSE OWENS.

I'm from a big family—the youngest of ten kids—
in a small town called Oakville, Alabama.

My real name wasn't Jesse.
It was James Cleveland Owens, though everyone
called me by my initials, J.C.

I was skinny as a kid, and sick a lot.

At five years old, I noticed a bump in my chest.

We lived really far from doctors, and even if we were close, we couldn't afford one.

My mother was one of the strongest and most determined people I knew.

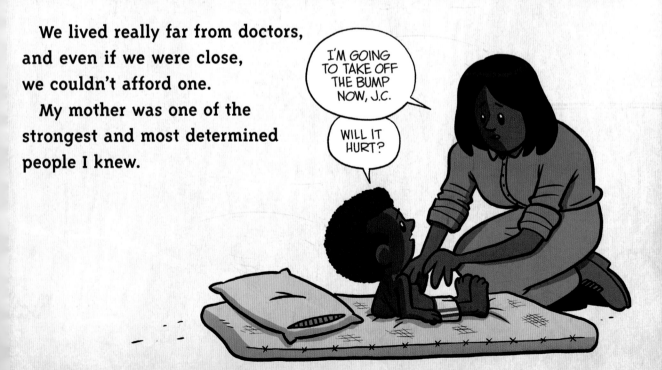

I remember seeing the tears in my dad's eyes.

It was one of the hardest moments of my life, but I got through it.

I ALWAYS SAID YOU WERE BORN SPECIAL.

MY SPECIAL BOY.

The next day, I was sitting up and eating.
The day after that, I was walking.
And the following day...

I was back working in the fields.
When I was a boy, my family farmed cotton.
My grandparents had been enslaved.
On these farms, life was hard.
Since we were Black, our only options were tough, low-paying jobs with no way to advance.

We were so poor, our house didn't have a proper roof or beds.

We couldn't even afford clothes.

One day, a landowner's son told me he dreamed of going to something called college.

He said it was a special school where you could be anything you want.

I told my family...

Dad ran like no one else.
Like a train blurring when it sped past.

He was the fastest in our county.

I wanted to be just like him.

Even as a boy, I loved running.
You could do it all by yourself. It didn't require money—just your own strength and determination.

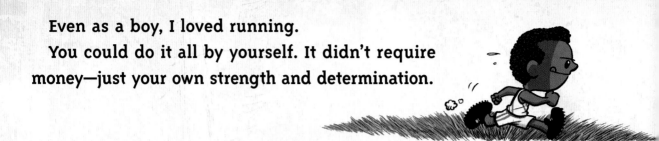

I was fast too.
When we played tag, no one could catch me.

When I was nine years old, my family left Alabama.
We'd heard stories about a place up north where Black people had more options.

My parents wanted us to get a proper education—so we'd have the opportunities they never had.

Where did we go?

Cleveland, Ohio.

It felt like a different world.

In school, my Southern accent was so thick, some teachers couldn't understand me.

The good news was, there were jobs for almost all of us.

My mom and sister cleaned houses, while I worked part-time shining shoes and pumping gas.

I also loved working at a greenhouse, tending baby oak trees.
I dreamed of one day having my own house with a big oak in front.

But no matter how hard we worked, money was always tight.

We couldn't even afford a Christmas tree.

My dad would get a free one after hauling away all the unsold trees.

EVERY YEAR, HE'D WORK ON THE HOLIDAY AND WE'D CELEBRATE CHRISTMAS A DAY LATE.

THERE WERE NO ORNAMENTS.

JUST THREE PIECES OF MOM'S JEWELRY AND OUR TATTERED CLOTHING.

THOSE SOCKS MAKE IT LOOK GOOD.

I had no idea it was all about to change.

I was never afraid of hard work.
Because of my after-school jobs, I could only train in the mornings.
Every day, we'd meet as the sun was coming up.

Coach would be by my side as I ran on the muddy track...

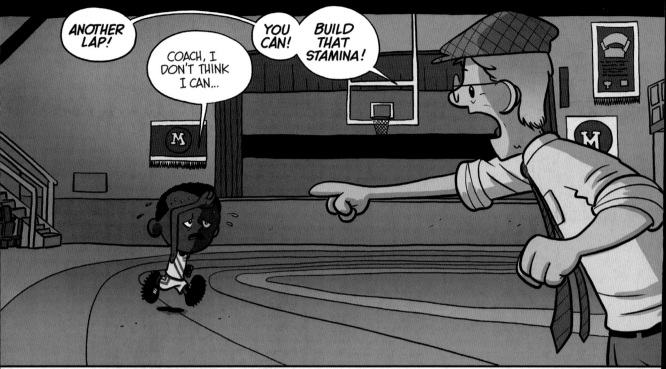

Even while I ran in place.

When I was fifteen, Coach Riley set up a hundred-yard dash on the sidewalk.

I ran it in eleven seconds, only about a second and a half shy of what was then the world record.

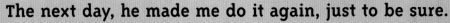

The next day, he made me do it again, just to be sure.

It was time for my first official race.

My lead didn't last long.

I was so focused on my competitors that day—and so upset.

But Coach Riley encouraged me.

By the time the race was finished, I'd come in fourth.

He was the first white man I really knew. He taught me how to be a better runner, and at a time when so many treated Black people differently, we treated each other equally and taught each other how to be better men.

Soon after, I was in a 220-yard dash.
Like before, I had an early lead.

And they still passed me by.

It wasn't enough.
I lost again.

To my surprise, Coach Riley was smiling.

CONGRATULATIONS.

FOR WHAT? I LOST.

This time, though, when I got tired, I realized I had more in me.

I dug deep. I pushed harder.

I was so frustrated, I kept running, even after the race was done.

NO. YOU DIDN'T.

EVEN WHEN THE RACE WAS OVER, YOU DIDN'T FOCUS ON THE OTHER RUNNERS.

YOU KEPT GOING.

THAT'S A WIN.

YOU OVERCAME YOUR GREATEST OPPONENT.

I knew what he meant. My greatest opponent was myself.

By age eighteen, I was one of the country's best sprinters and long jumpers.

But in the semifinal round to make it to the Olympics...

YOU GOT THIS, JESSE.

I lost again. I wasn't ready yet.

Here's the thing about losing:
It'll always teach you something.
That day, I saw the best runners up close.

They were human beings—just like me.
That meant they could be beaten.
Next time we raced, I'd make sure the crowd was cheering for *me*.

On June 17, 1933, I ran the hundred-yard dash in 9.4 seconds, tying the world record. From there, I finally made it to college— a place called Ohio State.

COACH LARRY SNYDER

WE'D LIKE TO MAKE YOU TEAM CAPTAIN, JESSE.

They'd never had a Black captain of a varsity team before.

That didn't mean I was suddenly treated fairly, though.
Black students weren't allowed to live in the best dorms...

THAT'S NOT FAIR.

or go to most nearby restaurants and movie theaters.

WHITES ONLY.

MOVI

NOW PLAYING!

Every day, my running gave me an opportunity.
But it didn't give me equality.

JESSE, I'M SORRY— I CAN'T LET YOU RUN.

BUT, COACH—

IF YOU HURT YOURSELF, IT COULD RUIN YOUR CHANCE AT THE OLYMPICS... AND ALL YOUR TOMORROWS.

I looked at him and said something I'd never said before.

WHEN YOU COME FROM WHERE I DO, YOU DON'T REALLY BELIEVE IN TOMORROWS.

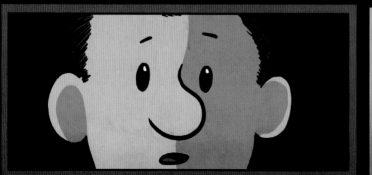

Coach knew I deserved my chance.

ONE RACE, JESSE.

THEN LET'S SEE HOW YOU FEEL.

I was in so much pain, they had to help me into my uniform.
But as any sprinter knows, the hundred-yard dash has a few key seconds.

The first is when you come out of the blocks.

The next is when you take those first strides into position.

But the most important is the last part of the race...

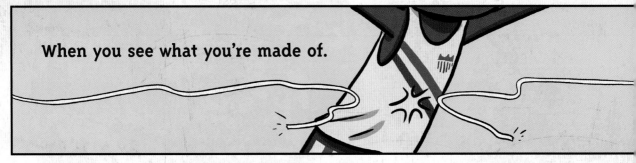

When you see what you're made of.

That day, in a single hour, I broke three world records and tied another in running, the low hurdles, and the long jump.

From there, I became one of the most famous runners in the country. But my hardest challenge was still ahead.

Back then in Germany, there were people known as Nazis who didn't like Black people, Jewish people, and other groups different from them.

The Nazis were led by a terrible man named Adolf Hitler who believed that white Germans were better than everyone else.

In 1936, his plan was to use the Olympics to prove it.

Most people on our track and field team were like me—poor Black Southerners.

Hitler hated us because of our skin color.

The German journalists wouldn't even use my name.

They thought their win was guaranteed.

They were wrong.

I thought the crowd would boo me.
But instead of cheering Hitler's name, they cheered mine.

The hundred-meter dash was the most prestigious track-and-field event. And I, a Black man, had won it in front of 100,000 white Germans.

100-METER DASH. GOLD MEDAL — 10.3 SECONDS.

INCREDIBLE!

Of course, there was one person who wasn't cheering.

Hitler refused to shake my hand like he did with other athletes.

Lucky for me, not everyone followed his example.

This is the best German long jumper: Carl Ludwig "Luz" Long.

Hitler called him a perfect example of Nazi superiority.

Yet when I jumped farther than anyone...

ANOTHER GOLD! JESSE OWENS SETS A NEW OLYMPIC RECORD!

LONG JUMP. GOLD MEDAL— 8.06 METERS.

We both knew Hitler was watching.

We knew the crowd was watching. That was the point.

Luz should've been my rival.

DON'T WORRY, LUZ.

A BLACK MAN WILL **NEVER** WIN.

He should've been my enemy.

Luz put his hand on my shoulder...

And congratulated me.

I put my arm around him.

Sports is about more than ability. It's about more than winning and losing. At its best, it's about character.

In my life, people thought less of me because of where I was born.
They counted me out because of the color of my skin.
But others pushed me to improve, helping me find my potential.
That's when I took off.

One day, you'll have your own races to run, your own hurdles to leap.
Just remember, it's not about how fast you go.
What matters is that you don't stop when it gets hard.
Dig deep, push yourself, and show what you've got inside.
When you do...

Life is not a sprint.

It's a marathon—a long-distance race that goes over hills and through valleys.

Here's the real secret: Don't focus on the finish line or what the other runners are doing.

Focus on doing right.
Focus on pushing hard.
Focus on your personal best.
That's where you see what you're made of.

Along your path, it'll be easy to find competitors.
It's better to find teammates.

I am Jesse Owens.
In the race of life, I defy expectations.

"Find the good. It's all around you. Find it, showcase it and you'll start believing it."
—JESSE OWENS

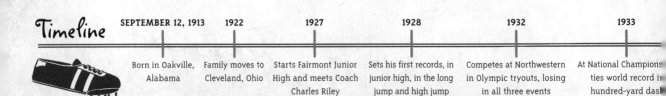

Timeline

SEPTEMBER 12, 1913	1922	1927	1928	1932	1933
Born in Oakville, Alabama	Family moves to Cleveland, Ohio	Starts Fairmont Junior High and meets Coach Charles Riley	Sets his first records, in junior high, in the long jump and high jump	Competes at Northwestern in Olympic tryouts, losing in all three events	At National Champions ties world record i hundred-yard das

Jesse Owens at the
1936 Olympic Games

Luz Long and Jesse Owens

1936 Olympics Medal
Ceremony

OCTOBER 9, 1933	MAY 25, 1935	1935	AUGUST 1936	AUGUST 5, 1976	MARCH 31, 1980
nrolls at Ohio State University	Breaks three world records in one hour in Ann Arbor, Michigan	Marries Minnie Ruth Solomon	Wins four gold medals at Berlin Olympics and sets three new world records	Is awarded the Presidential Medal of Freedom	Dies of lung cancer in Tucson, Arizona

For Scott and Lindsay Meltzer,
the other true athletes in our family,
for letting their little cousin win
–B.M.

For Mike Scopa,
a thoughtful, caring, and kind human being.
He may not run anymore, but he always inspires.
–C.E.

For historical accuracy, we used Jesse Owens's actual words whenever possible. For more of his true voice, we recommend and acknowledge the below works. Special thanks to Dr. Shaun M. Anderson for his input on early drafts.

....

SOURCES

Jesse: The Man Who Outran Hitler by Jesse Owens with Paul Neimark (Fawcett, 1978)

The Jesse Owens Story by Jesse Owens with Paul Neimark (Putnam, 1970)

I Have Changed by Jesse Owens with Paul Neimark (William Morrow, 1972)

Jesse Owens: An American Life by William Baker (Macmillan, 1986)

Triumph: The Untold Story of Jesse Owens and Hitler's Olympics by Jeremy Schaap (Houghton Mifflin, 2007)

FURTHER READING FOR KIDS

Who Was Jesse Owens? by James Buckley Jr. (Penguin Workshop, 2015)

What Are the Summer Olympics? by Gail Herman (Penguin Workshop, 2016)

I am Muhammad Ali by Brad Meltzer and Christopher Eliopoulos (Rocky Pond, 2022)

I am Jackie Robinson by Brad Meltzer and Christopher Eliopoulos (Rocky Pond, 2015)

....

ROCKY POND BOOKS
An imprint of Penguin Random House LLC, New York

First published in the United States of America by Rocky Pond Books, an imprint of Penguin Random House LLC, 2024

Text copyright © 2024 by Forty-four Steps, Inc.
Illustrations copyright © 2024 by Christopher Eliopoulos • Coloring by K. J. Díaz with Christopher Eliopoulos

Penguin supports copyright. Copyright fuels creativity, encourages diverse voices, promotes free speech, and creates a vibrant culture.
Thank you for buying an authorized edition of this book and for complying with copyright laws by not reproducing, scanning, or distributing any part of it in any form without permission. You are supporting writers and allowing Penguin to continue to publish books for every reader.

Rocky Pond Books is a registered trademark and the colophon is a trademark of Penguin Random House LLC.
The Penguin colophon is a registered trademark of Penguin Books Limited.

Visit us online at PenguinRandomHouse.com.

Library of Congress Cataloging-in-Publication Data is available.

Photo on page 38 courtesy of the IOC Olympic Museum/Allsport; medal ceremony photo on page 39 courtesy of Bettman; photo of Jesse running the 100 Meter race on page 39 courtesy of Popperfoto via Getty Images; photo of Jesse and Luz Long on page 39 by ullstein bild via Getty Images.

Manufactured in China • ISBN 9780593533369 • 10 9 8 7 6 5 4 3 2 1

TOPL

Design by Jason Henry • Text set in Triplex • The artwork for this book was created digitally.

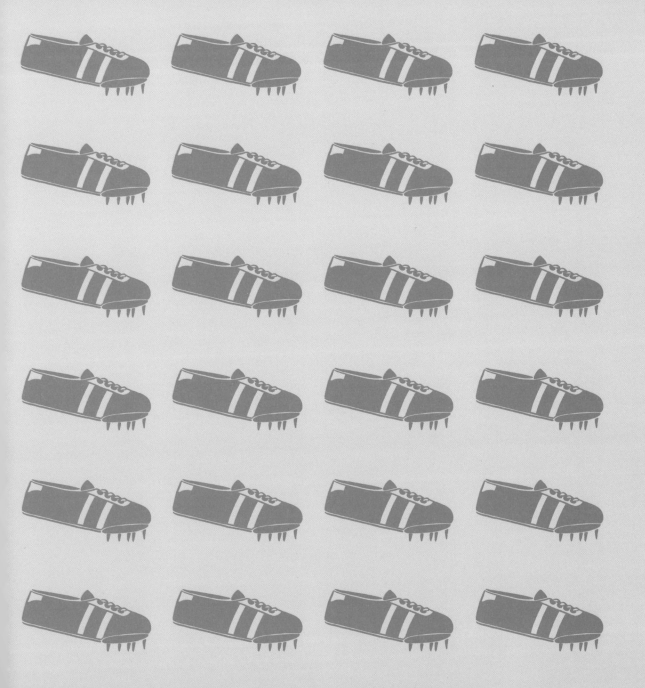

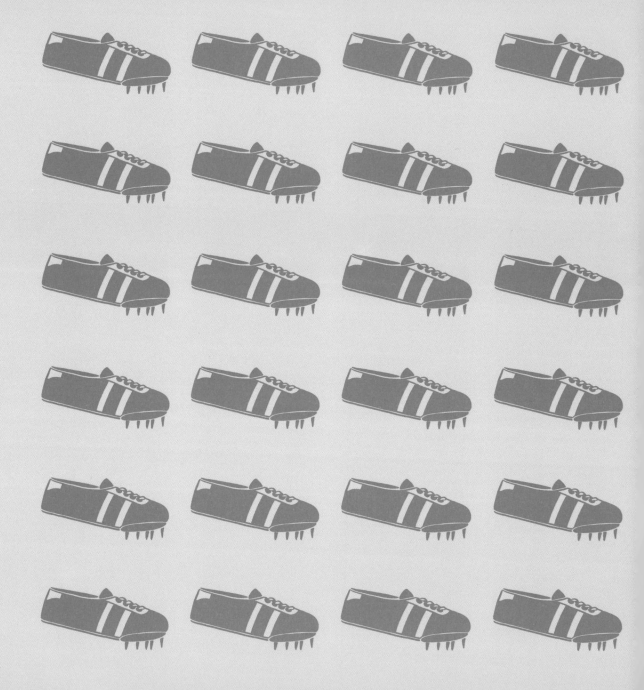